A SPIRIT DAUGHTER WORKBOOK

WRITTEN BY
JILL WINTERSTEEN

FOR TAURUS SEASON

APRIL 20TH – MAY 21ST

THE NEW MOON

FRIDAY, MAY 19TH

8:53AM PT

TAURUS SEASON

Each astrological season is an evolution of the one before it. Aries Season brought us fast-moving energy and new beginnings. As the Sun enters Taurus, life slows down. We are given space to feel, listen to our hearts, and let the seeds we created take form. As an Earth sign ruled by Venus, Taurus brings us foundational energy. With these vibrations, we can create anything we focus our attention on. This season is a time to find stillness, connect with the Earth around us, and feel the abundance already present in our lives. If Aries was a whirlwind of energy, Taurus is the calm after the storm.

Throughout this season, look for opportunities to uncomplicate your life, slow down, and find stillness. Taurus connects us with nature and reminds us that we are always supported by her strength. Step outside and feel the wind on your face, dip your bare feet in warm soil, and listen carefully to the song of the birds around you. Drop into pure presence by connecting with nature. Let this connection bring you back to the simple pleasures of life. Watch the Sun set, see the Moon rise, and lie beneath the stars. Allow these little moments to open your heart and remind you that you are held by the big Universe you are a part of.

TAURUS SEASON

As you find stillness and presence this season, also find simplicity. Taurus helps us simply find presence. This season is not about drama or turmoil. It is an opportunity to regulate your nervous system. Throughout this season, continually ask yourself what the simplest answer could be. Resist the urge to overthink things or spend too much time searching for logical solutions. Instead, tune into your instinct. Allow the answers you seek to appear, then trust them. Trust your intuition and trust that some things in life really can be easy.

As you find simplicity, you also find space. Without an overworking mind to complicate things, your feelings can breathe. You also can process past experiences and trauma. Taurus Season offers us a time to find the wisdom in life. It's a time to reflect from a safe distance on the road you've traveled. Without being immersed in your emotions or inner drama, you can find insights and the higher meaning to your journey. Taurus Season is a time to put some of the pieces together and understand your pain from a different perspective. It's a time to feel yourself in the present moment, where you can make sense of it all. Through this present awareness and reflection, you can heal. Taurus Season can be one of the most healing times of the year. This healing, though, is done through stillness, presence, and simple reflection. It's not a time to dig up old chaos. It's a time to be with what is occurring in each moment and feel your strength and resilience.

As you sit in the present moment, you can feel your inner peace and ability to weather any storm. You are your own rock. You can always rely on yourself, and you can always rely on nature around you. From this place of peace, you can take chances, leave your comfort zones, and forge a new path. Once you understand that you can always come home to yourself and always find the wisdom to heal your soul, your world opens up. You can find your creativity in the stillness of your mind. You can then share your creations with the world without fear of rejection. You can do something that scares you, but you know it is what your soul needs to grow. And you can take a leap of faith to build the life of your dreams. You can do it all because you know you have the greatest safety net of all: yourself.

It's from this inner reliance that abundance is born. When you have the inner confidence to take risks in your life, you can align with all forms of abundance. You find your passion and your creativity, then you pursue it without the fear of failure. When you align with your soul in this way, the Universe orchestrates itself to support you. Everything you need appears when you need it. And if it doesn't, you know that you can figure out your next step. When you believe that you can confront any adversity with courage, you take the leaps needed to create a life aligned with your heart and soul. You call in all forms of abundance to continually support your journey. You also realize how many energies you are already abundant in. Your life feels expansive and full of vibrations that support your body, mind, and emotions. It all starts with finding stillness, feeling your strength, and knowing you can rely on yourself.

Over this season, allow the rhythms of nature to bring you home to your stillness and peace. Feel your self-worth and know that you deserve everything you desire. You are worth slowing down for, and you are worth your full attention. Stay present with yourself and connect with the beauty around you. Experiment with tools that settle your nervous system and bring in frequencies that quiet your mind. Spend time with sound bowls or tuning forks. Experiment with new meditations or creative visualizations. Dedicate an afternoon to watching flowers bloom. Let these experiences open your heart, and feel rooted in your body. This season is a time to ground your energy and create a foundation that you leap from into any vision you wish to experience. Enjoy its simplicity and softness.

HOROSCOPES

YOUR RISING SIGN:

Your Rising Sign is the same as your Ascendant.

Often denoted as:
Asc
AC
Rising ↑

This is a point where the horizon line intersects a constellation.

In this specific chart the horizon line intersects Libra, making this person a Libra Rising.

You can look up your Rising Sign at astro-charts.com.

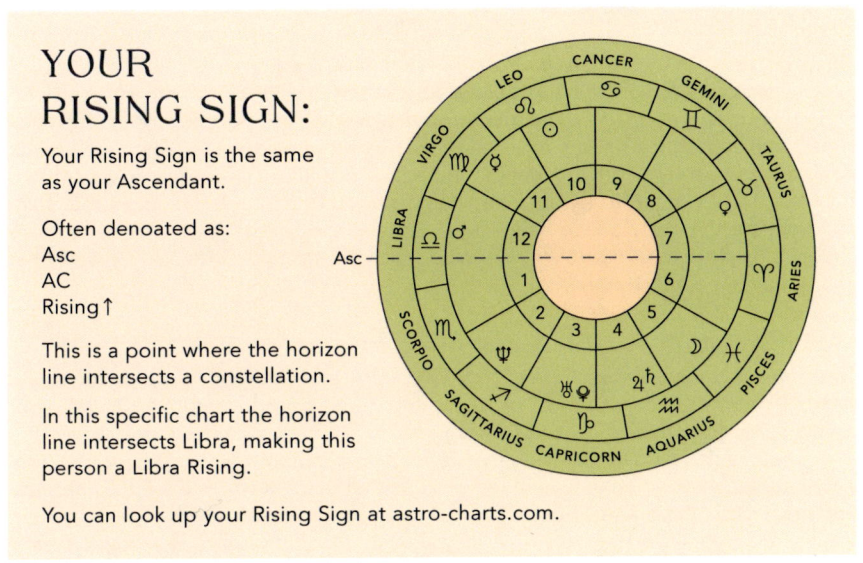

ARIES RISING:

This season challenges your definitions of resources and abundance. You don't always need security to charge forward, but it can be nice to know you have it. Over this season, lean into the energies that make you feel secure and confident in yourself. How can they help you build abundance? How can you view yourself as your most valued resource? Over the New Moon, consider writing intentions around your self-worth. Feel into your worthiness and create a vision that matches it. Know that you can begin anything with the right motivation and intent. Now is the time to create a life that feels stable, full of opportunity, and abundant in all ways.

TAURUS RISING:

This season is a time to feel into your self-worth and develop an identity that reflects it. Find stability and stillness through your deep connection with nature, and from there, decide what parts of yourself are ready for others to see. This is a time to define who you are in the world and what legacy you want to build. It's a time to show your creativity to others without fear and knowing you are worth all the applause coming your way. Over the New Moon, write intentions that reflect who you are ready to become. Feel into your self-worth and ask if your life matches that worthiness. If it doesn't, create visions that show a life that does. And feel your inner resolve to create this life in tangible form.

GEMINI RISING:

This season brings you in touch with your spirituality and offers a new perspective on it. Set aside time to experiment with new spiritual modalities that quiet your often overactive mind. Pay close attention to sound frequencies, incorporating sound bowls, tuning forks, and other vibrational tools of this type into your daily practices. Let these new spiritual paths open your mind and allow you to see yourself, your abundance, and your resources from a different point of view. On the New Moon, set intentions that open the doorway to new spiritual endeavors. See yourself evolving through methods of self-inquiry and reflection. Ask yourself what you are ready to begin, and dive in.

HOROSCOPES

CANCER RISING:

This season is a time to feel your inner stillness and ask yourself how you impact people around you with your stability. Spend time connecting with yourself and finding your center, then connect with others. Notice the people who match your vibrational frequency or are at least willing to meet you there. Also, notice the people who throw you off your center and be curious about why. On the New Moon, set intentions that reflect your inner leadership skills. Define practices that help you develop the inner peace needed to lead and the self-reliance it takes to make challenging decisions. It's your time to step into the spotlight and ask yourself what you need to feel ready.

LEO RISING:

This season brings a sharp focus to your career and life's work. If you're having internal debates around these topics, spend some time in nature to clarify your answers. Align with this season's energy to ensure that what you do for a living and what you're paid for these services matches your self-worth. Know that true abundance comes when you value yourself and all you have to offer. Focus on what you are most passionate about that feels like home to you. And if you're asking for less than your worth in any area of your life, use this season as a time to make adjustments where needed. On the New Moon, write intentions that envision you aligning with your life's work and carving out a career that feels like home. Begin a new path, if needed, or simply adjust the one you are already on.

VIRGO RISING:

This season disturbs your normal routines just enough to open your mind. Taurus Season is filled with possibilities for you. Take the opportunity to explore different areas of your town, expose yourself to new knowledge, or try a new hobby. If you've felt stagnant in any areas of your life, now is the time to shake things up a bit. On the New Moon, set intentions that incorporate different perspectives. See your potential, then ask yourself if you are dreaming big enough. Get out of your comfort zones and explore the unknown. Know you can always rely on yourself if things become challenging, and you can also return to your familiar routines for stability. Now is the time to adventure a bit and ask yourself to reach for a new reality.

LIBRA RISING:

This season brings a great time of personal growth for you. This growth, though, comes from slowing down, feeling your intuition, and making decisions from there. You may even feel an expansiveness to this season as projects and ideas accelerate to a new level. There is an abundance of transformative energy available to you right now, direct to the areas of your life where you want to make changes. As these changes unfold, allow them and allow yourself to grow where you need to accept a new version of yourself. On the New Moon, create intentions that include visions of an expanded version of yourself. What do you want to transform in your life this lunar cycle? Where do you need to grow? And what do you need to dissolve to allow this growth?

SCORPIO RISING:

This season brings a sharp focus to your relationships. It's a time to evaluate where you need adjustments in what you are giving and what you are taking within your partnerships. Before having any needed conversation, make sure to ground your

HOROSCOPES

energy by connecting with stillness. Sit in nature, find peace in your energy, and feel your strength. From this place, approach your partners and discuss what's in your heart. On the New Moon, make commitments to yourself from a place of self-worth. Then set intentions that hold space for relationships that match your self-worth to appear in your life. Be open to the unexpected this Moon and pay attention to who crosses your path. They might just have an important message for you.

SAGITTARIUS RISING:

This season brings attention to your offerings to others. It's time to feel your inherent gifts and share them with the world. First, though, align with this season's energy to find your inner stillness. From here, feel the energies that make you unique. Feel your creativity and decide how to materialize it in a tangible form. Then, align with your inner strength to show your inner world to others. Offer your gifts where they're needed the most, and know they will be well received. On the New Moon, create intentions that help you find your stillness, creativity, and inner resilience. Start on a path that helps you bring your ideas into form and give your unique talents to others.

CAPRICORN RISING:

This season offers lightness to your world. You tend to approach everything with a certain seriousness and project that as your identity. Taurus Season, though, asks you to breathe a little easier, connect with the gentleness around you, and lean on nature for some of the answers you seek. Slow down a bit this season, and nourish your spirit with play and spontaneous adventures. Feel your inner child and honor them with moment of pure joy. On the New Moon, create intentions that incorporate room for creativity, slower moments, and connection with your heart. Let the lightness of this season inspire you to laugh a little more, dance when you feel like it, and celebrate the small steps.

AQUARIUS RISING:

This season focuses your attention inward and allows some of your deeper feelings to arise. Align with Taurus to nourish your spirit and recharge your soul. Find solace in nature by slowing down to enjoy the sunset or moonrise, sip warm tea as you watch the dandelions grow, or find the present moment by walking on the Earth. Let the nature around you hold you, and in that security, feel your creativity blossom. Let it shine in every area of your life. On the New Moon, set intentions that reflect your center. Feel the truth of who you are and return home to yourself this New Moon. Let your intuition guide you to the answers you seek and hold space for creative solutions to appear that redirect your energy.

PISCES RISING:

This season brings your attention to how you exchange energy with other people and the world around you. It's a time to notice how you are always in communication with everything on an energetic level. Find your center and feel how you subtly influence everyone and everything through the energy you emit. Experiment with new forms of communication that ask you to expand your consciousness, including reiki, distance energy healing, and even body language. On the New Moon, create intentions that offer a new perspective. Feel how you have evolved this season on an energetic level and create visions that reflect your growth. Slow down and merge your energy with the New Moon and ask what it wants to teach you.

TIPS FOR TAURUS SEASON

CULTIVATING ABUNDANCE

We have a choice on how we view the world and the resources available to us. We can see the world as a place of scarcity, where there is not enough for everyone, or a place of abundance, where everyone can prosper. A scarcity mindset causes us to feel we have to compete for possessions, love, and even time. When we operate from a place of scarcity, we tend to regret missed opportunities, feel angry that we don't have enough, and envy others who appear to have more. A scarcity mindset can lead to depression, longing, and even guilt. If we manage to accumulate resources of some type, we may feel we don't deserve them over another person, leading to self-sabotage. A scarcity mindset tells us that we are not enough and will never have enough. This way of thinking limits us, our dreams, and our potential.

On the other hand, an abundant mindset teaches the opposite. This mindset assumes that there is always enough for everyone. There is always more love, more money, more time, and more resources. Most importantly, there is always more energy to create abundance in all forms. When we live from an abundant mindset, we have gratitude for what we have, cheer others on when they succeed, and trust the choices we make. We know that what is meant for us will never miss us and we are deserving of all we attract into our lives. Living from a place of abundance makes us feel joyful, inspired, grateful, and trusting. Our relationships improve, and instead of envying someone else, we know we can manifest any desire with intention.

Creating an abundant mindset can be challenging. We live in a society that operates from scarcity. We are constantly told there isn't enough, both personally and professionally. Everything from promotions to stock shares to health care is presented from a place of scarcity. Any time you hear there isn't enough ___, it points your attention to lack. Opposing these strong messages from external sources takes dedication and persistence. However, you can create an abundant mindset for yourself no matter what streams into your consciousness from the outside world. Each person who lives from and projects abundant energy shifts the collective. When more people think abundantly, it creates more abundance and changes the paradigm we all live under.

The Taurus Season is the perfect time to develop an abundant mindset. It's a time to focus on what you already have in your life and the energy you are already connected to, which can amplify. It's also a time to focus on what you love and can truly immerse yourself in doing. When you follow your passions, abundance follows you. When you focus on what you already have, abundance grows. And when you trust that everything you need will appear when you need it, it does. Most importantly, remind yourself over this season that you are worthy of abundance. You may need to do some internal work to discover why you may not think you are worthy of abundance. Self-worth is the key to creating a life of abundance. Once you feel you deserve your dreams, they materialize more easily. Below are some tips on how to create an abundant mindset this season and beyond.

DEFINE ABUNDANCE

What does abundance mean to you? How does it feel when you are abundant? Also, notice various forms of abundance. How are you abundant in love, resources, time, opportunities, knowledge, friendships, and gratitude? Where do you feel abundant in your life, and where do you feel lacking? Ideally, we want to feel abundant in every area since they feed into each other. We often, though, have a few places in life where we just don't feel there is enough. Notice what makes you feel abundant in those areas where you have enough, then become more aware of when and why you slip into a scarcity mindset.

TIPS FOR TAURUS SEASON

CULTIVATING ABUNDANCE

FOCUS ON THE GOOD

Throughout this season, focus on what you do have. Notice when your attention shifts to what you lack, and bring it back to all the good in your life. Become keenly aware of when you say or hear the phrase "not enough." Ask yourself if it is true and how you can shift to feel that there is enough. For instance, if you are looking for a new job, notice if you are telling yourself you don't have enough skills or don't know the right people, or there aren't enough jobs. Instead, focus on the skills you do have, the people you do know, and the resources available to you. A mindset is just that—a way to set your mind. Focus your attention on the good in your life, and more will always follow.

BE GRATEFUL

Along with focusing on the good, be grateful for what you have in your life. Gratitude is a powerful practice that can make what you have enough. It points your attention to the abundance already present and helps you create more. Gratitude practices come in many forms. You can start each day writing a simple list of gratitudes. You can also tell the people in your life what you appreciate about them each day. Even just thinking about what you appreciate about someone before a meeting can create an energy of abundance for both of you. Gratitude tells the mind that we have enough, we are enough, and there is enough for everyone. Commit this season to becoming abundant in appreciation and gratitude, which will bring you more abundance.

SURROUND YOURSELF WITH ABUNDANT-MINDSET PEOPLE

We become like the people we hang around. Our energy is contagious, and when we interact with others daily or even weekly, we take on their energy. To help you create an abundant mindset, surround yourself with people willing to think abundantly. This means people who cheer you on when you succeed and want to collaborate with you instead of competing for resources. It also means noticing when people repeatedly tell you there isn't enough of something and asking them to view a situation differently. When the people around you think abundantly, it can also help upgrade your mindset when needed. You can then do the same for others when they need an energetic boost.

TRAIN YOURSELF TO SEE OPPORTUNITIES

When we live from a scarcity mindset, we see limitations. We can miss opportunities right in front of us because we don't believe there are alternatives to the thing we are focused on. For instance, if you are focused on a past relationship and don't feel you are worthy of love because of it, you may miss opportunities to meet new people. Or, if you are focused on a financial situation you missed out on, you may miss an alternative that is available. Throughout Taurus Season, open your mind to see a bigger picture. Notice when you are hyper-focused on one thing or way of being and if it is limiting you in some way. Also, notice when you start saying things like "I can't do this" or "I missed the chance" or "That will never happen again." Start to rewrite your internal dialogue to reflect abundance and opportunities everywhere.

* You can learn more about creating an abundant mindset and releasing lack in the Abundance Course available on spiritdaughter.com.

TIPS FOR TAURUS SEASON

CULTIVATING ABUNDANCE

YOU ARE WORTHY

It's important to understand that your self-worth is the biggest block, or best facilitator, when it comes to attracting abundance. Your self-worth is what grounds you when negative thoughts come up. It creates your inner peace and reliance on yourself. Self-worth is a level above the temporary thoughts of the ego; it is connected to something higher: your true essence. Your sense of worthiness dictates what you can manifest in reality. If you do not feel good enough for a certain intention or dream, you won't be able to create it, no matter how many days you envision it. If you have trouble attracting any type of abundance, ask yourself if you feel worthy of receiving it and what thoughts are tricking you into believing you are unworthy. Feel into these answers and be honest with yourself. Know that you can shift your sense of self-worth through practice and commitment. Also, know that you are already worthy of anything you desire; you just need to realize it.

_____

_____

_____

_____

_____

_____

_____

_____

_____

_____

_____

_____

_____

_____

CRYSTALS FOR TAURUS

PINK OPAL is the stone of peace and tranquility. It brings about a feeling of calm, especially when painful memories arise. Hold a piece during meditation and allow its energy to softly heal old wounds that undermine your efforts to be still. Pink Opal is also wonderful to sleep with under your pillow if you have disturbing dreams or nightmares. It serves to gently soothe the soul and shift consciousness into a state of joy and creativity. Pink Opal is pink and cream.

Pink Opal vibrates to the mantra: "I am at peace."

LEPIDOLITE is an energetically stabilizing stone. It reduces anxiety by bringing us back to center and the source of our energy. In doing so, it helps us redirect our energy into something creative instead of something destructive. It reminds us of our divinity and our connection to the Earth, recalling that everything is happening as it's meant to be. Lepidolite is also an excellent stone to use when spacing out, as it can allow you to rest in stillness so you don't feel the need to do something. In this stillness, it can bring you to great truths. Lepidolite is lavender.

Lepidolite vibrates to the mantra: "I am still."

JADE is the stone of luck, manifestation, and abundance. It was once thought that anyone who touched jade was blessed for the rest of their lives. This belief is why it adorned so many kings and queens of centuries past. Jade soothes the energetic body and reminds us that we are inherently happy people. It allows us to let go of self-defeating thoughts and encourages us to create with our hearts. Jade also teaches us that abundance is always available and we never need to fear losing it. Place some in the money corner of your home, which is the farthest left corner of your house when walking through your primary entrance. Jade is light and dark green.

Jade vibrates to the mantra: "I am lucky."

PETRIFIED WOOD gives us grounding energy. It helps us form roots in our environment and reconnects us to those roots when we lose our connection out of fear or anxiety. Petrified Wood brings us the essence of the Earth herself. It also reminds us that there are things we can't control, and that's ok. As long as we stay grounded in ourselves, we can handle anything life throws at us. Petrified Wood is brown.

Petrified Wood vibrates to the mantra: "I am the Earth."

GREEN ONYX is a stone of abundance and fertility. It brings us the energy of new beginnings and helps us focus while we nourish this new energy. It is a calming stone that helps us tap into our seeds of creation and trust that we can nurture them to full bloom. Have some near if you are in the beginning stages of creation, especially if you doubt yourself. Green Onyx also protects against negativity, even if that negativity is coming from within. Have some near if you feel you are self-sabotaging your efforts with limiting beliefs. Green Onyx is light green with shades of cream.

Green Onyx vibrates to the mantra: "I am abundant."

TAURUS MEDITATION

EYEBROW
UNDER EYE
TOP OF HEAD
SIDE OF EYE
UNDER NOSE
CHIN
COLLARBONE
UNDER ARM
KARATE CHOP
SIDE OF HAND

Taurus energy is about feeling and physical touch. The following meditation incorporates touch as a way of breaking up stagnant energy in our body, so we are free to grow and evolve. EFT, or emotional freedom therapy, is a technique used to help heal and shift conditioned patterns through tapping on energetic points of the body. It is a simple meditation that can have profound effects on our energetic body by resolving issues buried in our subconscious layers.

Each EFT meditation consists of two sequences. The first sequence is designed to bring the underlying energy attached to a specific issue to the surface of your consciousness. This part calls hidden thoughts to the forefront of your mind, releasing them. The second sequence works to replace the old energies with new high vibrational affirmations. The first sequence clears out the old; the second replaces it with new, consciously directed energies.

EFT uses the points in the illustration to the left. You'll tap on these points with your index and middle fingers together as you say each statement below. Tapping occurs quickly, you'll tap once per second, for about 3-7 taps per point. You can tap with your dominant hand, on that side. If you're right-handed, tap these points on the right side of your face and body with the exception of the karate chop point.

The first EFT sequence is designed to release energies of unworthiness and insecurity. Our self-worth is the basis for all of our abundance. If we are to create a truly abundant life, it's important to become aware of and rid ourselves of feeling unworthy. It's also important to call out places we feel insecure so we can replace those feelings with supportive energy and reassuring affirmations.

Begin with the Karate chop point, which you tap on with four fingers. Tapping always starts at this point with three statements. Continue tapping through the rest of the points, then repeat the entire first round. Take a few deep breaths between sequences, feeling the energy start to shift. The second sequence is positive affirmation tapping. This part is designed to direct your energy toward creating vibrations of self-worth and abundance in your field.

TAURUS MEDITATION

PART 1

KARATE CHOP POINT

(SIDE OF THE HAND) Even though I am not in complete alignment with my self-worth, I choose to love and accept myself.

Even though I lose my center from time to time, I choose to love and accept myself.

Even though I've doubted my worth, I choose to change my programming and shift my energy toward abundance.

EYEBROW I don't feel worthy of abundance.

SIDE OF EYE I choose to value myself.

UNDER EYE I don't believe I can have everything I want.

NOSE Other people can have abundance, but I am not one of them.

CHIN And this causes me to doubt myself.

COLLARBONE And not accept myself.

UNDER ARM It also causes me to compare myself to others.

TOP OF HEAD And judge myself compared to them.

EYEBROW I live in a story that I don't deserve abundance.

SIDE OF EYE I don't feel worthy of everything I want.

UNDER EYE I have many reasons I am unworthy.

NOSE Some come from childhood.

CHIN Maybe I felt judged.

COLLARBONE Or was told I was unworthy.

UNDER ARM Or not good enough.

TOP OF HEAD And now I don't know how to choose abundance.

Repeat both sets (minus the KC Point). Take three deep breaths.

PART 2

The second sequence is positive affirmation tapping. This part is designed to direct your energy toward creating vibrations of self-worth and abundance in your field.

KARATE CHOP POINT Even though I have a story around abundance, I choose to completely love and accept myself.

Even though I have told myself lies about abundance, I choose to completely love and accept myself.

Even though I have not believed in my own worth, I believe in my power to rewrite my story around abundance.

EYEBROW Starting today, I choose to believe I deserve abundance.

SIDE OF EYE I choose to value myself.

UNDER EYE I am worthy of everything I deserve.

NOSE I am capable of creating abundance in my life.

CHIN And I deserve to have abundance come easily to me.

COLLARBONE I can choose to be abundant.

UNDER ARM I release all of my blocks around abundance.

TOP OF HEAD And allow myself to receive the energy of abundance.

EYEBROW I allow myself to feel good.

SIDE OF EYE And release the burden that I am not good enough.

UNDER EYE I choose to accept the truth that I am enough.

NOSE I no longer live in the lie that I am unworthy.

CHIN I am part of the beauty of the Universe.

COLLARBONE And I deserve to have everything I desire.

UNDER ARM I deserve to receive infinite abundance.

TOP OF HEAD I am in alignment with abundance.

Repeat both sets (minus the KC Point). Take three deep breaths.

TAURUS LUNAR FLOW

Taurus rules the throat, neck, thyroid, and vocal tract. During Taurus Season, we want to free up stagnant energy in these areas. The following sequence is designed to help you open up the areas ruled by Taurus to further align with her vibrations. You can practice this sequence every day during Taurus Season or just on the New Moon.

NECK STRETCH

Begin in a seated position with your neck and spine straight. You may sit on a pillow or block if you need to elevate your hips. Tip your head to the right, allowing your right ear to fall to your right shoulder. Take your right hand and gently press on the left side of your head, adding to the stretch. Breathe deeply here for 5 breaths, creating space between your left ear and shoulder. Carefully lift your head back to center and switch sides.

CAT/COW

Come to hands and knees. On inhale, arch through your spine, lifting your head. On exhale, round through your spine, and look at your navel. Continue this for 5 breaths, feeling your neck stretch and your throat open.

DOLPHIN POSE > CHILD'S POSE

Still on hands and knees, come down to your forearms. Have your elbows in line with your shoulders and your palms pressing flat on the ground. If you have very tight shoulders, place a block lengthwise between your forearms. Allow your neck to relax, and straighten your legs for Dolphin Pose, lifting your hips into the air. This is Downward-Facing Dog on your forearms. Press your heels toward the floor as you breathe into your shoulders. Send your breath in between your shoulder blades and continue to lengthen your neck. Take 5 breaths here, then lower down to your knees to Child's Pose for a few breaths.

WARRIOR 1 > HUMBLE WARRIOR

From the top of your mat, step your right foot back for Warrior 1. Have your back foot angled in at a 45° angle, and bend into your front knee. Reach your arms up toward the sky and square your torso to the front of the mat. Feel your heart expand with each inhale and your torso grow taller. Spend 5 breaths here, then clasp your hands behind you, opening your chest.

TAURUS LUNAR FLOW

On exhale, fold to the inside of your left leg, keeping your knee bent and your hips square to the front. Let your head and neck relax as you look toward your navel. Take 5 deep breaths here, feeling your chest expand and your legs strengthen. On inhale, come upright and step to the top of the mat. Repeat on the other side, then return to the top of your mat.

WARRIOR 2 > REVERSE WARRIOR

Step your feet apart three to four feet apart on your mat, facing the side of the room. Turn your left foot toward the back of the mat and angle your right foot to 45°. Bend in your front knee and reach your arms out to either side for Warrior 2. Reach actively through your fingertips. Feel the strength of your legs supporting you and ground down into the Earth. Breathe here for 5 breaths, then flip your front palm to the sky and lean back for Reverse Warrior. Stay bent in your front knee and stretch through your left side, reaching your left arm alongside your ear. After 5 breaths, return to center and switch sides.

BRIDGE POSE - 3X

Lie on your back with your knees bent, feet hips' width apart. Your feet should be close enough to your hips that you can gently brush your heels with your fingertips. On inhale, lift your hips, keeping your knees in line with your ankles. Shimmy your shoulders underneath you slightly so you can grasp your hands. Press down into your upper arms to help lift your chest higher. Breathe deeply into your lungs on each inhale. On exhale, lift a little higher in your hips. Stay here for 5 breaths before releasing. Repeat this two more times.

CAMEL POSE - 2X

Come to kneeling with your hips over your knees. Place your hands on your low back for support. Inhale, reach your chest to the sky, lengthening out your spine. As you exhale, slowly bend backward, keeping your back supported and your hips over your knees. On each inhale, reach through your chest. On each exhale, bend back a bit more. If it's comfortable, let your head fall back, opening your neck and your expression. Breathe deeply for 5 breaths, then return to kneeling. Sit back on your heels and observe your breath and the openness of your heart. Repeat once more.

SUPINE TWIST

Lie on your back. Hug your left knee into your chest, then twist to the right. Reach out your left arm and look to the left. Stay here for 5 breaths before switching sides. Feel your spine and neck open in this twist and feel supported by the floor beneath you.

SAVASANA

Lie flat on your back, with your palms facing upward in a receptive position. Close your eyes and allow your entire body to relax into the floor beneath you. Feel the openness you've created in your throat and neck. Breathe naturally here for 5 minutes.

Visit spiritdaughter.com/collections/zodiac-yoga to flow with our Taurus Zodiac Yoga video.

TAURUS X THE NEW MOON

MAY 19TH

The Taurus New Moon is full of intuition, femininity, and softness. All planets, except Pluto, land in feminine astrological signs. Many planets land in Taurus or make aspects to those in Pisces and Cancer. This Moon brings us a receptive energy to feel into, align with, and open ourselves to as we write intentions. As you journey through this New Moon, remember to allow. Let yourself simply be with the vibrations that are coming your way and rising up within you. Listen to the quiet whispers of your inner knowing and let go of the need to force anything. Instead, be with what is while silently knowing what is about to happen.

On this New Moon, we have the Sun, Moon, Jupiter, Mercury, Uranus, and the North Node in Taurus. We also have Saturn and Neptune in Pisces, and Mars and Venus in Cancer, bringing in the element of Water to our Earth Moon. Each astrological energy is either feminine or masculine. The feminine, or nocturnal, energies are the Earth and Water signs. The masculine, or diurnal, energies are the Fire and Air signs. This New Moon brings us an abundance of femininity, encouraging reception over action and introspection over external observation. It's a Moon for sitting in the quiet morning stillness and feeling the power of your intuitive knowing. It's a Moon to remember you already have the answers if you're willing to receive them.

As you work with this New Moon, feel the inner resources available to you. This Moon has the potential to help you tap into skills you already possess to create harmony and balance in your life. It's a time to envision a new version of yourself who remains calm in the face of adversity and knows how to handle any potential challenge.

TAURUS X THE NEW MOON

MAY 19TH

It's a reminder that you have every resource or tool you'll ever need to navigate life today, tomorrow, and the next day. Feel the resilience of your soul, the creativity of your energy, and the strength of your mind this New Moon. You already possess so many tools that help you find your center and hold on to it as life moves around you. These tools may look like mantras, breath work, sensory connection, trust, or inner knowing. They are always available to you at any moment once you remember that they exist.

When you fully understand that you have the inner resources to navigate any situation, you find it easy to leave your comfort zones and take chances that bring you into a life you love. You already possess many skills to calm your nervous system or process your emotions. Feel them this New Moon. Also, feel your confidence, courage, and fortitude, and start to view them as resources that can bring you back to peace when life takes twists and turns. Instead of worrying about what could happen or hesitating out of fear of the unknown, this New Moon asks you to feel your strength and excitement. Yes, you'll have worries, fears, and doubts, but you can go forward despite them. And even if your worst-case scenario comes true, you possess the ability to creatively problem solve and work your way into the best-case scenario.

This New Moon's message is loud and clear: do not fear the unknown. Fear not finding your potential. As the Moon and Sun sextile with Neptune in Pisces, you are reminded to receive your dreams. Spend time today doing nothing, daydreaming, and being open to hits of inspiration. Let visions arise in your consciousness, and be curious about them. Let yourself become swept away by your dreams and feel into them. Image they are real and let yourself experience them in your body, emotions, and energy. Most importantly, be open to signs and messages coming to you today. Look around a bit more than you usually do. Keep your eyes open for messages that inspire your imagination and remind you to listen to your dreams.

The New Moon also forms a sextile aspect with Mars in Cancer today, bringing us more water to worth in our intentions. Mars brings us to our passions in Cancer, and on this New Moon, it reminds us to be open to new passions rising up from our intuition. Perhaps there is something we desire in our lives but have been afraid to pursue. This Moon is the time to acknowledge your fear, learn from it, but take away its control. It's a time to leave the comfortable and familiar and instead seek the thing that makes you feel alive. Perhaps your heart will race, or you'll feel a mixture of fear or excitement. This is how you'll know you're on the right track. Feel your inner resources that help you put your fears aside, let go of hesitation, and remember that you can face anything with courage. Feel the tools you can rely on to quiet your heart and envision yourself as happy, calm, and ready.

As your ride the beautiful vibrations of this New Moon, feel your potential to create the life you deserve. This creativity is already within you. It belongs to you, and so do your dreams. This New Moon is not about doing. It's about showing up, connecting, and receiving the answers. It's about following the path of your intuition, knowing that it will always lead you to where you need to be. You do not need to worry about the details or fear the unknown. All you need to remember is that you are always worthy of your dreams. You are worthy of abundance in all forms, and you already possess every resource you need to make your visions materialize.

SETTING UP FOR MAGIC

When setting up a Taurus New Moon Circle, choose a space that feels grounded, supported, and secure. This space can be inside or out, as long as it feels like a safe container for your explorations. When choosing your space, observe how it makes you feel and select items to use that make it feel balanced and beautiful to your energetic body. This may mean organizing the existing space in a new way, or cleaning out some clutter if you are choosing a room inside your home. It may even mean rearranging furniture or gathering a few new plants that add fresh energy into the space. A day or two before the New Moon, if possible, pick your space, so you have time to plan how you want to shape it. You can, of course, spontaneously pick up this workbook and practice the rituals at any time in any place, and the energy of the Moon will still be available to you. The below guidelines are for enhancing the energy a bit with items that align with the energy of Taurus.

Taurus, like all zodiac signs, carries inherent energy. With this energy comes colors, shapes, scents, and elements which match its vibration. Think of these items as energetic mirrors placed around the room to amplify and direct the energy. Use your intuition to guide you in choosing items for your circle. If you a beautiful banquet of flowers calls your attention, consider incorporating them. If a crystal is seeming extra shiny and bright, use it in your circle, or if you attracted to a certain scent, consider using it a diffuser or through a candle. For Taurus vibrations, think spring. Bright greens flowers fully in bloom, and the scent of wood enlivened by the rain. Below are some suggestions and directions on colors, shapes scents, and textures that align with Taurus.

Once you've chosen your space, imagine a white light creating the boundary of the circle and place candles, crystals, and other items within this boundary. Place a crystal, candle, or another piece of magic in the center to give structure to the circle. This is also where you can set up a crystal grid to help direct the energy further. If you are creating an altar, you can place it in the easterly corner to help call in the energy of new beginnings. Know that your attention and awareness of the energy available is the most important thing for working with it. You can practice the exercises in this workbook in any way you choose; you can practice alone, on a train, or in a group of people around a bonfire. Your willingness to open up, to look within, and expand your consciousness is the most important piece to this day.

As much as possible, incorporate all these elements into your circle. Use candles for Fire, a room diffuser or spray for Air, the crystals and flowers to represent Earth, and have some water in a metal bowl. Once you set up your circle, cleanse the space with sage or palo santo. After the circle is cleansed, smudge yourself and your friends before they enter the circle.

You can begin the circle by acknowledging everyone in the room. You can then continue to the yoga, if you are practicing, and then the meditation. Once you feel the room is centered, begin to talk about the astrology of the night and what it means for each of you. If it is a larger circle, you may want to designate a talking stick or crystal to give to each guest while they speak. After you've shared your understandings, continue with the questions and the journaling portion in this workbook. After everyone has finished, talk again about your experiences with the energy and the revelations which may have occurred. You can share as little, or as much as you like with the group. Never feel obligated to speak; sometimes energies need time to develop before they are brought to the light of day.

SETTING UP FOR MAGIC

FOR YOUR ALTAR OR MOON CIRCLE

FLOWERS: Peonies, Poppies, Foxgloves, Forget-Me-Nots, Jade

SCENTS: Cedarwood, Eucalyptus, Fresh Linen

SHAPES: Cube

TEXTURES/FABRIC: Light Woods, like Oak or Birch

COLORS: Greens, Mustard Yellow, Light Turquoise

ELEMENTS: Wood, Flowers

At this point, you may also pull some cards to help tune further into your intuitive guidance. You can use tarot cards, goddess cards, animal medicine cards, or any other decks that may be in your toolkit.

Once you've finished the circle, close it by having everyone close their eyes and meditate on what they are grateful for tonight and every night. You can even practice being grateful for things that haven't come your way yet. Gratitude will attract them to your energetic field and let the Universe know you are ready to receive them. Enjoy this time to be with your self, your heart, and your soul. Get to know yourself on a deeper level and allow your life to unfold another layer each New Moon.

and just when you least expect it,

the storm passes.

- spirit daughter

NEW MOON QUESTIONS

These questions are designed to help you become clear in your intentions. Take a few deep breaths to ground yourself before answering them. Sit with each question for a moment and allow the answer to naturally arise, being open to the person you are becoming. As you write, know you are opening the door to your intuition and giving permission to your highest visions to come out and be seen.

1. How does your life reflect your self-worth?

_____

_____

_____

_____

_____

_____

_____

_____

_____

_____

2. What abundance is already present in your life?

_____

_____

_____

_____

_____

_____

_____

_____

_____

_____

_____

3. What brings you into the present moment, where everything feels still and you can find inner peace?

_____

_____

_____

_____

_____

_____

_____

_____

_____

_____

_____

_____

4. What helps you tap into your inner resources and feel strong and capable of coming up with creative solutions?

_____

_____

_____

_____

_____

_____

_____

_____

_____

_____

INTENTION SETTING

Before writing your intentions, tap into the abundance you already have in your life. Feel into the energies already present and be grateful for them. Abundance comes in so many forms. You might be abundant in creativity, time, intuition, knowledge, friends, love, nature, present moments, and so many other things. Make a list of everything you are already abundant in, then write your visions for the next six months. See what you already have and what you want to add to your life. Incorporate the leaps you need to take and the resources you'll need to confidently step into your dreams. Then notice if those resources are already within you and ask yourself how you can enhance them.

This is also a New Moon for being receptive. Allow your visions to find you. Do not force them or chase them. Let them arise naturally without much thought. With all the feminine energy present on this Moon, emotions are heightened. Feel your intentions through your intuition. Even if they don't make sense right now, or you have no idea about how you will manifest them if they come up in your consciousness, explore them. Sit with yourself, sit with nature, and let yourself simply be this New Moon. In this being, let your visions come to you. Ask yourself what you desire most. Ask yourself what you are holding yourself back from and who you would be without any fear. Start with these questions to prompt your visions, then continue as your intuition guides you.

As your visions unfold, see the life coming to you. Know that it is already yours. You already are connected to every energy you desire. The key is to focus on how these vibrations are already present in your life. See yourself living your highest vision. See your day and feel the emotions and energies your life brings you. Use all of your senses to experience this vision. Notice smells, sounds, and tastes. How does your life feel to your hands? How does it sound? What colors and scenes of nature are you experiencing? Let visions run through your consciousness, and choose their direction. Watch them evolve, and let your intuition direct them when needed.

Write your visions in detail, not concerning yourself with the steps you need to take to get there. Instead, trust that you are worthy of these visions and they already belong to you. Trust that if they are coming to you, they are meant for you. And be grateful for all that you already have in your life. Be grateful for every piece of abundance available to you, and know that when you are grateful, the Universe knows you are ready for more.

_____

_____

_____

_____

_____

_____

_____

_____

_____

INTENTION SETTING

AFFIRMATIONS

Affirmations can become powerful resources to tap into when life brings us challenges. Review your intentions and visions created. Notice any doubts, fears, or indecisiveness that arises when thinking about your visions. These energies will hold you back from taking needed steps to materialize your intentions. They will also keep you in a lower vibration, unable to attract the higher vibrations needed to manifest your visions.

Write down any fears, doubts, or insecurities about your visions. Do you believe they can come true? Do you believe you can manifest them? What about them scares you the most?

Now write down affirmations in the form of powerful "I am" statements that you can return to when your fears or doubts arise. What can you say in moments of doubt? What can you say to yourself when things don't go as expected? What can you say when you're scared that things won't work out? What can you say when you're scared they will?

+ FEARS, DOUBTS, INSECURITIES

_____

_____

_____

_____

_____

_____

_____

_____

_____

+ AFFIRMATIONS / MANTRAS

_____

_____

_____

_____

_____

_____

Taurus

CREATIVITY. STILLNESS. BEAUTY. GROUNDING.

PERSONAL SIGNS

TAURUS SUN

People with their Sun in Taurus are the creators of the zodiac. They are artists, painters, and musicians who draw energy from the stillness of their mind. They are deeply connected to nature and feel the rhythm of the Earth through their entire body. They must be mindful to nurture this connection often and stay grounded.

Taurus Suns move through the world with all of their senses. They like to see, touch, hear, taste, and smell things. They experience the world fully and immerse themselves in every intimate detail. The use of their senses helps keep them in the present moment and stay connected to their body and breath. Taurus Suns need to feel their feet on the ground, or they quickly lose their footing and can end up ungrounded, full of anxious thoughts.

An ungrounded Taurus Sun is much like a bull in a china shop. They run from idea to idea, never committing to one thing and causing havoc all around them. They lose touch with their body and get lost in the thoughts of their mind. Without stability, Taurus Suns find it challenging to create and find worth in their creations. The best remedy for a Taurus Sun who is feeling insecure and uncentered is Mother Earth. A hike in the woods, time on the beach, or Savasana in the grass is all they need to reconnect with nature and themselves.

It's also important for Taurus Suns to remember their worth and walk through life with the inner knowledge of how valuable they are in this world. They must be mindful not to get caught up in the rat race of collecting material possessions and find solace in their own inherent value. Their greatest resource is themselves. Taurus Suns have the power to create any form of abundance through their self-worth. When they genuinely value themselves and their creations, they have the ability to call in abundance easily and with little effort.

TAURUS MOON

People with their Moon in Taurus crave security. They are on a journey this lifetime to understand that nothing in life is certain except for their own breath. Taurus Moons can suffer greatly from anxiety, always feeling insecure and unsupported. They may even find themselves constantly worried about financial resources, looking for outside support instead of support from within themselves.

Taurus Moons benefit greatly from times of stillness and meditation. They need a feeling of contentment and peace to feel emotionally stable. Like Taurus Suns, they need to connect with nature when they feel lost or unbalanced. Even if they are city dwellers, it's important for them to travel to nature, or they may feel restless and unhappy. When they connect with the Earth, they find security in their heart, and all of their anxious thoughts quiet down to low whispers. They may even find they fade away completely.

When a Taurus Moon feels grounded in their energy, they can fully connect with their body. Their love language is touch, and they need to lean into this sense when sharing intimate moments with others. They communicate through their fingertips and need partners who understand that sometimes no words are needed.

Taurus Moons also have a stubborn heart, which is a good thing! Taurus Moons stay true to what they love against all the odds and are a shining example of perseverance in the face of adversity. They tend to commit for life and may even find they stay in a relationship long past its expiration date. They need to be aware of remaining in relationships out of habit or comfort and must break away if the partnership is no longer helping them grow. Growth is pivotal for a Taurus Moon. They must always be willing to leave their comfort zones for the limitless potential of the unknown.

ASTROLOGY FORECAST

APRIL 21ST - MAY 20TH

APRIL 21–MAY 14: MERCURY RETROGRADE IN TAURUS

Mercury stations retrograde today until May 14, breaking the streak of planets moving forward since January 22. When planets start stationing retrograde, it feels like the entire cosmos slows down. You may feel the brakes being applied to situations or projects as the Sun moves into Taurus, and Mercury starts peddling backward in the sky. Take this downshifting as encouragement to sit with yourself and have a conversation. Mercury Retrograde enhances our ability to communicate with ourselves. Spend time journaling, preferably within nature, during this retrograde. Connect with the Earth to feel your stillness. And if something breaks, see it as an opportunity to recharge through a walk, hike, swim, or something else that makes you feel connected and alive.

APRIL 27: FIRST QUARTER MOON IN LEO

As the Sun squares the Moon today, we have our First Quarter Moon in Leo, reminding us of our strength and ability to face any problem. Leo is the brave-hearted lion of the zodiac, who rules with an open heart and a touch of humor. Leo is a queen who teaches us that we need no one's approval but our own. Feel into this energy today and over the next few days. Feel your courage and your compassion as we journey through the beginning days of Taurus Season. What does this Moon want to tell you? How can you find stillness and connect with the Earth while nurturing your heart? Furthermore, how can the combination of heart and inner peace help you build your dreams?

MAY 1 – OCTOBER 10:
PLUTO RETROGRADE IN AQUARIUS & CAPRICORN

Pluto stations retrograde today until October 10 in Aquarius. Pluto will return to Capricorn on June 11, where it will end its retrograde. Pluto's short stint in Aquarius is a preview of a larger, twenty-year energetic shift about to take place in 2024. With its retrograde and return to Capricorn, we are seeing our last few years in review. This retrograde is a time to process transformations that have taken place in the last three years. You may experience memories resurfacing around pain, trauma, or other life cycles. This retrograde is an opportunity to reprocess the past. Pluto is the planet of transformation. It reminds us that we are part of a larger cycle of energy that spans many lifetimes. During Pluto Retrograde, we are asked to look inward and process our pain and even trauma through a different lens. Pluto Retrograde is about profound transformation to restore power and control in our lives. It is a time to go inward and break free of manipulative behavior to reclaim ownership of our energy. It is also a time to transform trauma into places of power through deep healing. Pluto Retrograde asks, "How can your pain turn into fertilizer?" Pluto Retrograde's crystal is Tourmaline.

MAY 5: SCORPIO LUNAR ECLIPSE

Please refer to the Scorpio Lunar Eclipse workbook

ASTROLOGY FORECAST

APRIL 21ST - MAY 20TH

MAY 7: VENUS ENTERS CANCER UNTIL JUNE 5

Venus, the planet of love and beauty, enters Cancer until June 5. Venus is a divinely feminine sign, and, in Cancer, it highlights the power of intuition. Spend time over this transit feeling the beauty of your inner knowledge. Communicate with people who uphold the feminine energy, learning from them as you get in touch with your own sacred power. This may mean finding a feminine teacher or spending time understanding your feminine lineage. Learn about your femininity and become curious about how it impacts your life.

MAY 12: LAST QUARTER IN AQUARIUS

Today the Moon lands in Aquarius for our Last Quarter Moon, a time of release. Aquarius reminds us that not only air connects us, but so do our thoughts and our energy. It is the sign of the collective consciousness. Depicted as the water bearer, Aquarius connected cultures and brought water to various tribes. With water, she brought new ideas, different perspectives, and innovative problem-solving.

When the Last Quarter Moon lands in Aquarius, it's an opportunity to break free of your habitual responses, patterns, and addictions. It's a time to change your way of thinking with the help of others. Your support can come in the form of people or energies you can connect with through intention. Spend some time tonight thinking about where you feel stuck or stagnant. Is there something you to change but just can't seem to make the shift? Write down your support and reach out to your network, even if they reside in the ethers. Be open to receiving inspiration, even from the air you breathe.

MAY 16: JUPITER ENTERS TAURUS

Jupiter enters Taurus today for the next year. Jupiter generally remains in a sign for twelve months, setting the tone for how we feel about abundance, our potential, and expansion. With Jupiter in Taurus, we feel expanded. This transit reminds us that we are secure, and it encourages us to take leaps of faith to meet our potential. It asks where in our lives we are selling ourselves short out of fear of the unknown. It also redirects our attention to tangible forms of abundance we can rely on that are already present in our lives.

Over this transit, slow down, enjoy life, and let your expansion unfold. Be patient with yourself and know that you can never miss your fate. This is a time to let your creativity blossom through connection with nature and others. Collaborate over ideas and let shared experiences bring you joy, serendipity, and openness.

MAY 20: MARS ENTERS LEO

Mars, the planet of passion, enters Leo until July 10. Mars in Leo lights a fire under our quest to understand ourselves. It's a time to feel into who you are and bravely fight for that person. Burn away anything that blocks you or prevents you from showing your true colors to the world. With confidence, be yourself in all circumstances, and if someone doesn't approve of you, kindly step away. Know that this transit is a fiery one and can bring up anger and frustration. If you are experiencing these emotions, ask yourself how you are not aligning with the real you. Have you hidden out of fear or some other reason? How can you get back to your authentic truth? And because it's Leo, how can you have fun doing it?

UP NEXT

GEMINI SEASON

MAY 21ST

The lively energy of Gemini Season is on the horizon. Expect the element of air to expand your curiosity and lift your visions to new heights.

HAPPY
NEW MOON!

Thank you to everyone who supported and purchased this workbook.

Special Thanks to Rebecca Reitz (rebeccareitz.com, @becca_reitz) for her beautiful artwork on the cover & pages 2, 4, 8, 18, 28.

For a monthly subscription contact hello@spiritdaughter.com or visit www.spiritdaughter.com.

Disclaimer: The exercises and yoga sequences in this book are physical activities that should be performed carefully to avoid injury. You agree to accept all risks and release Spirit Daughter and any guest instructors from any and all liabilities. Please take care and enjoy.

Follow along our journey on IG:
@spiritdaughter

We always love seeing your photos & hearing about your experiences with the workbooks! Tag us to be featured on our community page:
@spiritdaughtercollective